Contents

What does being
    responsible mean? 4

Ways to be responsible........... 6

Activity...................... 22

Picture glossary 23

Index 24

Being responsible means you
do the right thing without
being asked.

Being responsible means taking
charge of what you do.

When you tidy your room
without being asked to ...

you are being responsible.

When you put on your seat belt
without being asked to ...

you are being responsible.

When you feed your pet without
being asked to ...

you are being responsible.

When you look after your little
brother without being asked to …

you are being responsible.

When you throw away rubbish
without being asked to ...

you are being responsible.

When you brush your teeth
without being asked to ...

you are being responsible.

When you admit that you made a mistake ...

you are being responsible.

It is important to be responsible.

How can you be responsible?

Activity

How is this boy being responsible?

Picture glossary

admit tell something that you may be afraid to tell

responsible able to be trusted; taking care of yourself, your toys, and the people around you

Index

look after 12

mistake 18

pet 10

rubbish 14

seat belt 8

take charge 5

teeth 16

tidy 6

Note to Parents and Teachers
Before reading
Explain that when someone asks them to do something and they do it sensibly and carefully, they are being responsible. Sometimes they might see that something needs to be done and go and do it, for example tidying up – then they are being very responsible. Ask the children if they can think of something they have done that shows how they are responsible – perhaps they looked after a baby brother or sister, watered some plants etc.
After reading
• Ask the children if they can remember their telephone number. Talk about telephone numbers they might need to know. Explain that they are responsible for trying to remember important numbers. Let them role play using the telephone to phone their own home.
• Play at crossing the road. If possible, place traffic lights in the playground or give one child circles of red, green, orange and ask the rest of the children to be responsible for taking their friend, or toy, across the road. The 'circle' child holds up the traffic light and the others have to look to see if it is green and then look left and right and decide if there is any traffic before they cross. Some children could be the traffic and ride appropriate vehicles.

Heinemann LIBRARY

Cassie Mayer

Being Responsible

Citizenship

www.heinemann.co.uk/library

Visit our website to find out more information about Heinemann Library books.

To order:
- ☎ Phone 44 (0) 1865 888066
- 📠 Send a fax to 44 (0) 1865 314091
- 💻 Visit the Heinemann Bookshop at www.heinemann.co.uk/library to browse our catalogue and order online.

First published in Great Britain by Heinemann Library, Halley Court, Jordan Hill, Oxford OX2 8EJ, part of Harcourt Education. Heinemann is a registered trademark of Harcourt Education Ltd.

© Harcourt Education Ltd 2007

First published in paperback in 2008

Editorial: Cassie Mayer and Charlotte Guillain
Design: Joanna Hinton-Malivoire
Illustrated by Mark Beech
Art editor: Ruth Blair
Production: Duncan Gilbert

Printed and bound in China by South China Printing Co. Ltd.

ISBN 978 0 431 18676 4 (hardback)
11 10 09 08 07
10 9 8 7 6 5 4 3 2 1

ISBN 978 0 431 18684 9 (paperback)
12 11 10 09 08
10 9 8 7 6 5 4 3 2 1

British Library Cataloguing in Publication Data

Mayer, Cassie
Being responsible. - (Citizenship)
1. Responsibility - Juvenile literature
I. Title
179.9

A full catalogue record for this book is available from the British Library